Japanese ORIGAMI

* PAPER PACK *

More than 250 Sheets of Origami Paper
in 16 Traditional Patterns

STERLING INNOVATION
New York

STERLING INNOVATION
New York

An Imprint of Sterling Publishing Co., Inc.
1166 Avenue of the Americas
New York, NY 10036

ISBN 978-1-4351-6452-9

Distributed in Canada by Sterling Publishing Co., Inc.
c/o Canadian Manda Group, 664 Annette Street
Toronto, Ontario, Canada M6S 2C8
Distributed in the United Kingdom by GMC Distribution Services
Castle Place, 166 High Street, Lewes, East Sussex, England BN7 1XU

For information about custom editions, special sales, and premium and corporate purchases,
please contact Sterling Special Sales at 800-805-5489 or specialsales@sterlingpublishing.com.

Manufactured in China

2 4 6 8 10 9 7 5 3 1

www.sterlingpublishing.com

Cover design: Elizabeth Mihaltse Lindy
Japanese patterns: Depositphotos, Shutterstock

CONTENTS

ORIGAMI SYMBOLS

VALLEY FOLD:
Fold paper forward

When you open paper that has been valley-folded, you will see a concave crease that bends inward like a groove, or valley. This is called a valley crease.

Fold away from you (mountain fold) and in direction of arrow.

MOUNTAIN FOLD:
Fold paper backward

When you open paper that has been mountain-folded, you will see a convex crease that bends outward—it has a little peak you can pinch. This is called a mountain crease.

Fold and unfold

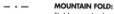

Fold toward you (valley fold) and in direction of arrow.

Insert

Unfold

Cut along line

Curve paper (soft crease)

X-ray view

Turn model over from one side to the other

 Rotate paper one-half turn (top of model will rotate to bottom)

 Scale of drawing enlarges

 Rotate paper one-quarter turn (top of model will rotate to side)

 Repeat here

 Rotate paper one-eighth turn (top of model will rotate to side)

6-8 Repeat step 6 through 8 here

 90° Form a right angle

 Match the dots

Push here

Raw Edge

Crease

Folded Edge
Back Layer

Double Raw Edge

 Hold here

Back Layer
Front Layer

5

BASIC FOLDS

BOOK FOLD

Fold one side edge over to lie on opposite side edge.

DIAPER FOLD

Fold one corner to lie over opposite corner.

CUPBOARD FOLD

Fold two opposite parallel sides toward each other to meet at center.

ICE CREAM CONE FOLD

Fold two adjacent sides to meet at center.

HOUSE ROOF FOLD

Fold two adjacent corners to meet at center.

BLINTZ FOLD

Fold all four corners to meet at center.

Note: Although less easily recognizable, the crease pattern for a sideways ice cream cone fold is still called an "ice cream cone fold." The same is true for all the basic folds.

Still an ice cream cone fold.

Still a book fold.

Still a cupboard fold.

REVERSE FOLDS

INSIDE REVERSE FOLD

In order for you to perform a reverse fold, your model or portion of model should have a front layer, a back layer, and a folded edge or spine connecting the two layers. In a reverse fold, an end of this double layer of paper is turned either into itself (inside reverse fold) or around itself (outside reverse fold).

1 You may wish to prepare your paper first by performing a simple valley fold that will serve as a precrease.

2 Check to be sure this is the shape you would like the paper to ultimately take, then unfold.

3 Spread the layers of your paper apart. Apply pressure (push in) at the mountain folded edge (spine) until it changes to a valley fold. At the same time, the precreases you made earlier will both become mountain folded edges.

4 This shows the inside reverse fold in progress. Keep applying pressure to end of paper until model can be flattened.

5 One end of your double layer is now "sandwiched" between the front and back layers.

OUTSIDE REVERSE FOLD

Again, starting with front and back layers connected by a "spine," you can "wrap" one end around both layers, as if turning a hood onto your head.

1 Mark the place where you want the fold to be (precrease). Unfold.

2 Spread the layers apart and wrap end around outside of model.

3 Press flat.

FOLDING HINTS

- It is usually easier to fold paper on a hard surface such as a table.

- Fold as neatly and as accurately as you can.

- If the paper you are using is colored or patterned on one side only: origami directions usually specify which side should be facing up when you begin folding. If this is not indicated, it is usually safe to begin with the white side of the paper facing you.

- It is usually easier to fold paper by bringing an edge from the lower part of the paper up. If you find it easier to fold this way and directions indicate a side-to-side or downward fold, you can always rotate your paper so that the direction of the fold is now upward, and then fold. After folding, reposition your paper so that it looks like the next step in the diagram.

- It is usually easier to make a valley fold in your model than to make a mountain fold. A valley fold becomes a mountain fold when you turn your paper over, so if a diagram indicates to make a mountain fold, you may choose to turn the paper over and make a valley fold. When you turn your paper back to the right side, you will see the desired mountain fold.

- Origami diagrams are usually drawn as if the paper were held loosely rather than pressed flat. This slightly three-dimensional representation is used to give you information about the different layers of paper. If you see a slight gap between edges in a diagram, this would disappear if model were pressed flat.

- In general, your paper should be folded right to an edge or crease, *without* leaving a gap, unless otherwise indicated in the written instructions.

FOLDING A CRANE

1 Bring bottom raw edge up to meet top raw edge. When edges and corners meet exactly, run your hand along folded edge to form a sharp crease. The fold you made is called a book fold.

2 Rotate your paper so the folded edge is now vertical.

3 Unfold—open the book.

4 Book fold and unfold: You should have a crease marking the vertical center line of your square. Bring the raw edge now at the bottom of your square up to meet the top raw edge. Crease and unfold.

5 You should now have two intersecting valley folds on the white side of your paper. These two creases should look like a plus sign.

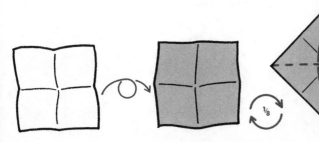

6 Turn your paper over to the colored side. The two creases you just looked at should now appear as mountain folds. Position your paper so it appears diamond-shaped. One corner of the square will be nearest to you.

7 Diaper fold: Bring bottom corner up to meet the corner at the top of the diamond. When both corners are precisely aligned, run your hand along the folded edge and make a sharp crease. Your paper should now have the form of a triangle.

8 Rotate your triangle so the folded edge that was at the base is now at the side.

9 Open the triangle.

10 Diaper fold and unfold: You should have a valley fold connecting the top and bottom corners of your diamond shape. Now make a crease connecting the two side corners of the diamond. Bring the bottom corner up to meet the top corner and crease at the base of the triangle. Unfold your paper.

11 Turn the paper back over to the white side and position so one edge is near you. The four creases you have just made should intersect at the center of your square and form a star. Hold your paper loosely; do not flatten. You should be able to see the pattern of the creases that radiate from the center as alternating mountain fold, valley fold, mountain fold, valley fold, etc.

This alternating crease pattern should give your paper a spring, or tension. Place your finger in the very center of the square (where all creases intersect), and push the center point down. As you push in one direction, the four corners of the square should pop in the opposite direction. Leave the center pushed down, and the four corners should be pointing up.

12 Using both hands, push all four corners of the square together at the same time.

13 Your paper should resemble a flower bud, open on top and closed at the bottom. You should see four flaps extending from the central axis of your model. Flatten the model, bringing two flaps together on each side.

14 Rotate your model so that the closed end is now at the top, and flatten.

15 You should have two flaps at each side of a diamond-shaped square. This is called a *preliminary base* because it is the basis for making many origami models.

16 You should have two flaps (a front and a back flap) on each side of the preliminary base. Bring the double raw edges from one front flap over to sit on the center line. Repeat on the other front flap.

17 You have made an ice cream cone fold with the front layers of your model. Fold the top triangle ("ice cream") down, using the top of the "cone" as your guide.

18 Leaving the triangular flap folded down, unfold the ice cream cone creases made in step 16.

19 There are several layers of paper exposed at the bottom of the model. Lift up the bottom point of front layer only. Swing point all the way up as far as you can—the fold you made when you turned down the "ice cream" will be your guide. (The triangular flap will also swing up.)

20 The front of your model will look like a boat. Bring the long side edges of the boat (raw edges) together so they meet each other and sit on the vertical center line. Make sure the top and bottom points are even. Run your finger around the folded edges to sharpen.

21 Bring the top point down to the bottom of the model.

16-21

22 Turn the model over and repeat steps 16 through 21 on the back.

23 This is a completed bird base. It is so called because the traditional Japanese crane, and many other models, can be folded from this base.

This drawing is a combination of steps 26 through 29.

24 Make sure the split in the diamond shape is pointing toward you. Fold the lower edges (front layer only) inward to almost touch the vertical center line. Turn the model over and repeat.

25 The two points at the top of the model are wings. The two sharp "spikes" at the bottom will be inside-reverse-folded up and between the wings to become a neck and a tail. To simplify the inside reverse fold . . .

26 . . . fold the front layer at the right over to the left, as if turning the page of a book.

27 Lift the bottom point up to the top.

26-29

28 Turn the left page (front layer only) back to the right. As you do so the "spike" will be sandwiched in between the wings.

29 Before you flatten the front and back layers, pull the "spike" slightly out to the side and set it in this position by pinching the base of the wing. Repeat steps 26 through 29 on the left.

30 Inside-reverse fold the tip of one slender point to form a head.

31 Spread the wings apart.

32 Hold each wing close to the central triangle. Gently pull your hands apart, causing the triangle to spread and flatten.

33 Your crane model is complete.

FOLDING A MASU BOX

Box Bottom

1 Begin with the colored side of the square facing up. Book fold and unfold (twice): fold and unfold the square in half in both directions. If you do not want these creases to show on your finished box, crease only near the side edges of the square and leave the middle uncreased. Each long "pinch" should be approximately one-fourth the length of one side.

2 Turn your paper over to the white side. Blintz fold: use the creases from step 1 as a guide to fold all four corners to the center.

3 Cupboard fold and unfold: bring the top and bottom edges inward to meet at the center. Crease sharply and unfold.

4 Cupboard fold and unfold: bring the right and left sides inward to meet at the center. Crease sharply and unfold.

5 Unfold the top and bottom triangular flaps.

6 Refold on the existing creases that connect the far dots. Crease sharply and then partially unfold so that the two flaps stand at a right angle to the rest of the model. They form two sides of your box.

7 For this step you will be folding simultaneously on three existing creases: push inward on the small mountain-fold creases where the color and white meet. At the same time, valley-fold on the crease that connects these two mountain folds.

8 You should now have your box. Grasp the long tab that sticks up and pull it down and inside the box so that it lines the inside.

9 Repeat step 8 on the other open end of your box.

10 Reinforce the creases on the finished box.

Box Lid

11 Use a square the same size as the square you used for the Masu Box. Follow the instructions for the box but replace steps 3 and 4 with the following:

12 Fold the bottom edge up to lie approximately 1/8" below the center. The size of the gap may vary from 1/16" to 3/16", depending on the thickness of the paper you are using. Crease sharply and unfold. Repeat on all four sides on the blintzed square. Continue from step 5 of the box. Fit the finished lid over the box bottom.

OPTIONAL BOX "TRICKS":

• To keep the four flaps that line the inside of your box from "popping" up, lift the flaps up for a moment and place a small piece of tape, sticky side up, in the center of the box. Replace the flaps so that they stick to the tape and also cover it so it is hidden from view.

• For an extra-sturdy box, cut a piece of cardboard to fit in the bottom. Unfold the box back to step 7 and insert the cardboard under the two bottom flaps. Then refold the box and the cardboard will be hidden.